ideals
VALENTINE

More Than 50 Years of Celebrating Life's Most Treasured Moments

Vol. 52, No. 1

*"Oh, if it be to choose and call thee mine, Love,
thou art every day my Valentine!"*

—*Thomas Hood*

IDEALS—Vol. 52, No. 1 February MCMXCV IDEALS (ISSN 0019-137X) is published eight times a year: February, March, May, June, August, September, November, December by IDEALS PUBLICATIONS INCORPORATED, 565 Marriott Drive Suite 800, Nashville, TN 37214. Second-class postage paid at Nashville, Tennessee, and additional mailing offices. Copyright © MCMXCV by IDEALS PUBLICATIONS INCORPORATED. POSTMASTER: Send address changes to Ideals, PO Box 148000, Nashville, TN 37214-8000. All rights reserved. Title IDEALS registered U.S. Patent Office.
SINGLE ISSUE—$4.95
ONE-YEAR SUBSCRIPTION—eight consecutive issues as published—$19.95
TWO-YEAR SUBSCRIPTION—sixteen consecutive issues as published—$35.95
Outside U.S.A., add $6.00 per subscription year for postage and handling.

Printed and bound in USA by The Banta Company, Menasha, Wisconsin. Printed on Weyerhaeuser Husky.

The paper used in this publication meets the minimum requirements of American National Standard for Information Sciences— Permanence of Paper for Printed Library Materials, ANSI Z39.48-1984.

Unsolicited manuscripts will not be returned without a self-addressed, stamped envelope.

ISBN 0-8249-1123-7

Cover Photo, VALENTINE ROSES,
Larry LeFever, Grant Heilman Photography

Inside Front Cover,
ST. VALENTINE'S GREETING,
Fine Art Photographic Library Ltd.

Inside Back Cover,
LOVE AMONG THE ROSES,
Fine Art Photographic Library Ltd.

My Valentine

Lucille Crumley

I found it today in a box put away
With letters faded and brown;
With a fan and a bow from the long ago,
A flower, and a blue silken gown;

Not a treasure of art, just a wreath on a heart
And a verse on a rose-bordered page;
A bit of the past that went by too fast—
A valentine yellowed with age.

With a sigh and a smile, I held it awhile
From the dark of its scented retreat.
Those days were fair, those hours so rare;
The first love of youth is so sweet.

I found it today put gently away
And remembered the day that it came.
I bent lightly to press one more caress
Where my love had written his name.

Thou Art Not Lovelier Than Lilacs

Edna St. Vincent Millay

Thou art not lovelier than lilacs—no,
Nor honeysuckle; thou art not more fair
Than small white single poppies—I can bear
Thy beauty; though I bend before thee, though
From left to right, not knowing where to go,
I turn my troubled eyes, not here nor there
Find any refuge from thee, yet I swear
So has it been with mist—with moonlight so.
Like him who day by day unto his draught
Of delicate poison adds him one drop more
Till he may drink unharmed the death of ten,
Even so, inured to beauty, who have quaffed
Each hour more deeply than the hour before,
I drink—and live—what has destroyed some men.

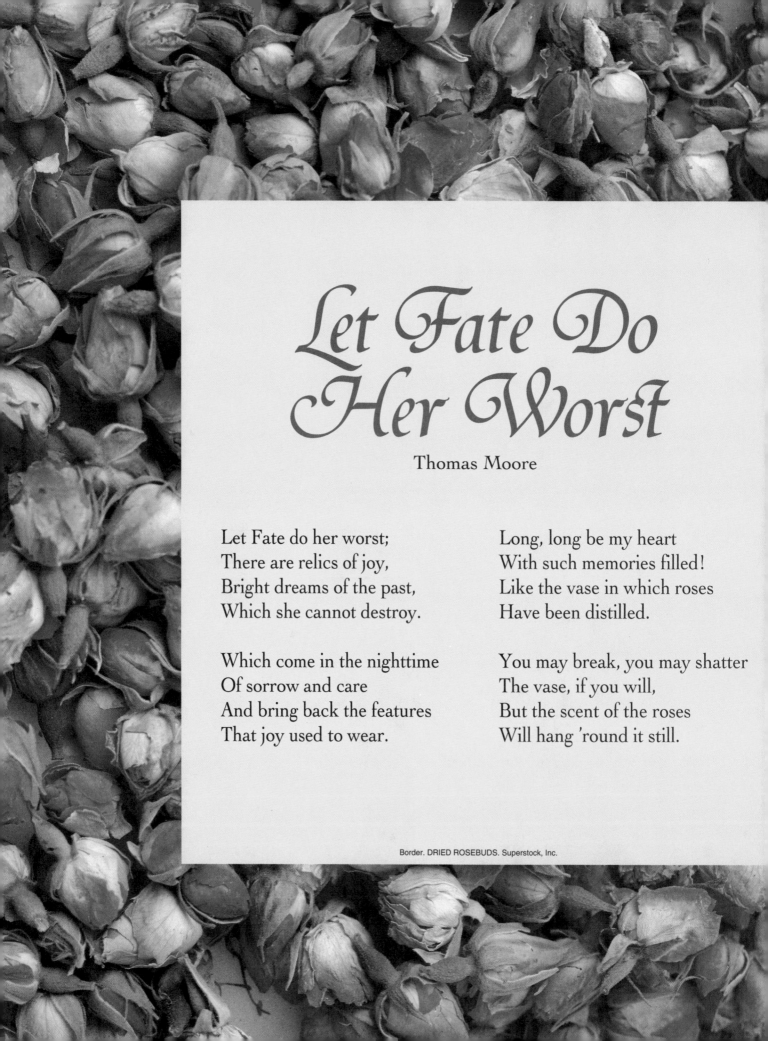

Let Fate Do Her Worst

Thomas Moore

Let Fate do her worst;
There are relics of joy,
Bright dreams of the past,
Which she cannot destroy.

Which come in the nighttime
Of sorrow and care
And bring back the features
That joy used to wear.

Long, long be my heart
With such memories filled!
Like the vase in which roses
Have been distilled.

You may break, you may shatter
The vase, if you will,
But the scent of the roses
Will hang 'round it still.

A PERFECT BLOOM. Bruce Curtis Photography.

$Strange$ that such a little rose should live on for well-nigh half a century, calmly putting forth its leaf and bloom summer after summer, whilst so many of the men and women who knew it once have passed away. It somehow makes me think of the old monk, pointing to the frescoes on his convent walls and saying, *"These are realities, we are the shadows."*

E. O. Boyle
Diary

BITS & PIECES

Love is the poetry of the senses.
It is the beginning, the middle,
and the end of everything.
Travis Henderson

Love is a gift that may only be shared
by those who would give it away.
Lovetta Bennett

Love is the light and sunshine of life.
We cannot fully enjoy ourselves, or anything else,
unless someone we love enjoys it with us.
Lord Avebury

Love is a circle that doth restless move
in the same sweet eternity of love.
Robert Herrick

Love is indestructible;
Its holy flame forever burneth;
From heaven it came, to heaven returneth.
Robert Southey

Love is the golden chain of eternity, linking yesterday,
today, and tomorrow into an everlasting bond.
Fern H. Hunt

Love is a many-sided sacrifice.
It means thoughtfulness for others;
it means putting their good before self-gratification.
Love is impulse, no doubt;
but true love is impulse wisely directed.
H. R. Haweis

Love is a beautiful flower that blossoms on earth,
with its roots embedded in eternity.
Marvea Johnson

Love is of God; and every one that loveth
is born of God, and knoweth God.
He that loveth not knoweth not God;
for God is love.
I John 4:7–8

What's in a name?
That which we call a rose
By any other name
Would smell as sweet.

—William Shakespeare
Romeo and Juliet

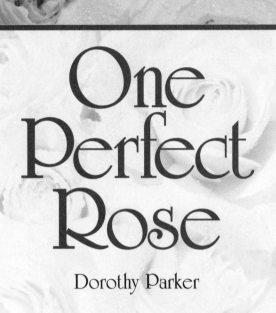

One Perfect Rose

Dorothy Parker

A single flow'r he sent me, since we met.
All tenderly his messenger he chose;
Deep-hearted, pure, with scented dew still wet—
    One perfect rose.

I knew the language of the floweret.
"My fragile leaves," it said, "his heart enclose."
Love long has taken for his amulet
    One perfect rose.

Why is it no one ever sent yet
One perfect limousine, do you suppose?
Ah no, it's always just my luck to get
    One perfect rose.

Handmade Heirloom

Judith Baker Montano

SAMPLES OF SILK RIBBON EMBROIDERY. Photograph from *The Art of Silk Ribbon Embroidery* by Judith Baker Montano. Photograph courtesy of C&T Publishing, © Copyright 1993. All Rights Reserved.

SILK RIBBON EMBROIDERY

*J*ust the word ribbon conjures up beautiful visions: little girls with flowing hair ribbons, mothers in dressing gowns decorated with silk ribbons, presents wrapped in satin ribbons. Silk ribbon embroidery, as the name implies, is embroidering with pliable, bias silk ribbon in widths varying from four to seven millimeters. With care, satin ribbon, polyester ribbon, and even spark organdy can be used to highlight your work. The narrower the ribbon, the smaller the finished work.

Today, the interest in Victoriana and days gone by attests to the renewed popularity of silk ribbon embroidery. Women are interested in Victorian needlework and decoration, which makes the art of silk ribbon embroidery a perfect choice.

In considering the types of heirlooms you would like to embroider, observe everything around you. You may choose to express yourself with an embroidered pillow, sachet, bandbox, picture frame, vest, or even a wedding gown. Personally, I love to garden; it is therapy for me. During a silk ribbon embroidery lesson, my friend gave me food for thought. She told me to look in my own garden for inspiration—and she was so right! There's nothing like being on your knees, hands in the dirt, nose to nose with your flowers!

Another good design idea is to mix silk ribbon embroidery with other embroidery techniques such as punch needle embroidery, crewelwork, or cross-stitch. Also, painting techniques should not be overlooked. By using dyes, acrylic paints, watercolors, gouache paints, or colored inks, a background can be painted directly onto the base fabrics.

If you love the time-treasured look of the Victorian period, first choose an appropriate background fabric such as moiré, silk taffeta, or velvet and use silk ribbons in muted, dusty tones that appear soft and grayed. Silk threads can be used to further highlight your embroidery by working them into flower centers, stems, leaves, and berries.

A common misconception is that the silk ribbon roses and other flowers are created separately and then sewn onto the fabric with traditional thread, but this is not the case. Silk ribbon embroidery is exactly what the name says: It is the art of embroidering with silk ribbons instead of thread. The needle is literally threaded with ribbon and the ribbon is taken in and out of the fabric.

Chenille and tapestry needles are the only types of needles used in silk ribbon work. Traditional threading methods allow for a stitch that locks the ribbon into the eye of the needle and makes a soft knot at the end of the ribbon. Use a short length of ribbon (twelve to sixteen inches) as you work to make the ribbon easier to manipulate. If the ribbon is pulled too tight or if it twists too much, it will just look like a heavy thread.

Silk ribbon can be embroidered on a variety of fabrics, such as velvet, linen, moiré, taffeta, organza, and knit. The fabric should have a weave sturdy enough to support the embroidery, but not so stiff that it shreds the ribbon. Keep in mind at all times that silk ribbon embroidery is delicate and soft. It cannot stand up to a lot of wear. Decide right from the start whether the item is to be washed or dry-cleaned and how much abuse it will receive. Also, it is a good idea to test all fabrics, ribbons, and threads for colorfastness before you start your project.

So many different stitches are employed in silk ribbon work that it is highly recommended you purchase a good book or learn directly from a friend who has already mastered this beautiful craft. Some examples of the various stitches include the straight stitch, cross-stitch, lazy daisy stitch, whipped running stitch, feather stitch, and French knot.

The little-known art of silk ribbon embroidery, also called ribbon work and Rococo embroidery, actually has nearly a 300-year history. It first appeared in France during the Rococo era of the 1700s. From 1750 to 1780, fashions called for elaborate dress decoration of ribbons, flowers, and ruching applied by embroidery. Royalty and court ladies wore gowns festooned with silk ribbon embroidery.

Only royalty and the court could afford to wear such elaborate garments. These were produced by "official" embroidery houses and took months of labor. Soon French court fashion drifted to England, and silk ribbon embroidery became a fashionable statement for the ladies of the British court. From there it moved to British colonies such as the United States, Canada, Australia, and New Zealand.

The 1880s and 1890s saw the most extensive use of ribbon work on ball gowns and elaborate evening costumes. Usually antique pastels in color, the embroidery resembled the costume embroideries of eighteenth century France. Pale rose, dusty rose, sage green, faded purple, and pale pink-violet were the most popular colors. Ribbon work was applied to cuffs and collars of children's dresses as well as to adult costumes. Favorite flowers were the heartsease, fuchsia, convolvulus, and moss rose.

Picture a young girl close to your heart dressed in a white silk organdy dress accented with delicate silk roses, forget-me-nots, and daisies—a timeless heirloom to pass down through the generations—and all embroidered by your hand. Silk ribbon embroidery is very exciting and rewarding. The stitches can be easily mastered and look more intricate than they are. Like any craft, it takes time and practice. One final admonition: This beautiful embroidery technique is highly addictive. Once you start, you may find yourself embroidering everything!

Judith Baker Montano is the author of The Art of Silk Ribbon Embroidery, *published by C&T Publishing, P.O. Box 1456, Lafayette, California 94549. Judith has won many awards for her fiber art and teaches throughout the United States, Canada, Australia, New Zealand, and Japan.*

Valentine Memories

Shirley Sallay

Grandma's book of valentines
    Rekindles memory's flame,
Of days when she was just a girl
    And life a happy game.

Each lace-edged card a greeting bears
    From friends of long ago,
Girls in gingham dresses
    And that "special" Sunday beau.

It brings a twinkle to her eye,
    Dissolving lines of age,
As we sit in the lamplight
    And turn each well-worn page.

It makes me kind of wonder
    If perhaps some distant day,
A grandchild shall sit at my side
    And leaf each page this way.

'Cause I could sit for hours,
    There at my grandma's knee,
And listen to the stories
    That the valentines set free.

A book of antique valentines
    That reaches back in time
To tell the tales of yesteryear
    In illustrated rhyme.

My Love

Harold F. Mohn

When all the flowers have faded
And fallen fast away,
You'll find my love unchanging
And constant each new day.

When all the leaves have left the trees
And left them standing bare,
My love will still be vibrant
And just for you to share.

When snow and cold pervade the air
And wintertime is here,
My love will always keep you warm
And fill your heart with cheer.

COLLECTOR'S CORNER

Lisa C. Thompson

A COLLECTION OF FANS. Bruce Curtis Photography.

FANS

Fans speak the language of love. Women of the Elizabethan and Victorian eras learned to manipulate their pretty fans for silent but effective communication with their suitors. A fluttering fan under smiling eyes was clearly a positive message, whereas a fan snapped quickly shut told a young man just when he'd made a mistake. The art of fluttering a handheld fan served as a silent form of communication between couples in a strict, formal society. One of the most romantic, flirtatious, and creative tools used for silent wooing was the folding fan. In fact, complicated languages developed using the folding fan.

Two different types of fan language emerged during the eighteenth century. One involved painstakingly spelling out words with special placements of the fan. A faster method developed in Spain in which entire words or phrases could be expressed by a single movement of the fan. Books were published that taught young women how to use the fan language. For example, a woman seen twirling the fan in the left hand was really telling her admirer "We are watched." Fans were often referred to as "feminine weapons" because as a woman wielded her folding fan, she was deftly pulling the heartstrings of her admirers.

If a young woman fluttered one of the popular conversation fans, a young man could choose from one of the thirty questions printed on one side and the woman could choose from one of the thirty replies on the opposite side. The questions and answers were silly and trivial, but afforded young people an acceptable way to flirt and communicate somewhat privately in an era when marriages were arranged and conversations monitored by everyone in the drawing room.

Fans were used long before the parlor room games of the Victorian era. Fans date back to c. 1350 B.C. Egypt when two ostrich-feather fans were placed in the tomb of Tutankhamen. The folding fan didn't originate until the ninth century. A Japanese legend tells of a man who was fascinated with the fold of a bat's wing and recreated it in the form of the folding fan. This Oriental novelty made its way to the West via Chinese and Portuguese merchants in the sixteenth century. One of the most famous portraits of Queen Elizabeth I was painted by M. Gheeraerts the Younger in 1592 and shows her holding an Asian folding fan.

By the mid-seventeenth century, every Western woman considered a folding fan an essential part of her attire. Subjects pictured on the leaf of the fans (the flexible, pleated material that unites the rigid framework of the fan) included paintings of scenes from literature and the Bible, maps, riddles, advertisements, political propaganda, and even the latest dances. Paintings of current events were also popular, such as the launch of the first hot air balloon in 1782. Fan styles mimicked fashion, changing from large to small to complement a woman's dress.

When evaluating antique fans, collectors should always choose fans that have been or could be carefully restored. Quality handwork as well as exotic materials such as ivory, bone, horn, and tortoiseshell also add value to fans. A collector can identify a machine-made fan, popular after the industrial revolution, by the stamped designs instead of hand-carved details on the fan's sticks, which comprise the rigid framework of the fan.

The three types of fans are fixed, folding, and brisé. A fixed fan, often called a hand-screen, is a rigid fan that is usually oval or round and mounted on a handle. Hand-screens were used during the winter months to protect a woman's hands from the fire. Pleated folding fans open to varying degrees, with the cockade folding fan opening to form a complete circle. Folding fans should always be opened from left to right. A brisé fan is a fan with no leaf but consists of rigid, overlapping sticks held together at the base by a rivet and the top by a ribbon or cord.

Fan collectors often specialize by choosing feather fans, commemorative fans, Oriental fans, or even advertising fans. Some collectors do not recommend framing a fan because it can cause the sticks to warp and the leaf to lose its elasticity and ability to fold.

Fans represent a bygone era of romance and intrigue to which collectors are irresistibly attracted. A collection of fans can be a history lesson told through fine art, printed advertising, or even lace and silk. A beautiful fan might also serve as the perfect valentine for the special someone who pulls at *your* heartstrings.

The First Day

Christina Georgina Rossetti

I wish I could remember the first day,
First hour, first moment of your meeting me;
If bright or dim the season, it might be
Summer or Winter for aught I can say
So unrecorded did it slip away,
So blind was I to see and to foresee,
So dull to mark the budding of my tree
That would not blossom yet for many a May.

If only I could recollect it, such
A day of days! I let it come and go
As traceless as a thaw of bygone snow
It seemed to mean so little, meant so much;
If only now I could recall that touch,
First touch of hand in hand—did one but know!

We Met on Roads of Laughter

Charles Divine

We met on roads of laughter,
    Both careless at the start;
But other roads came after
    And wound around my heart.

There are roads a wise man misses,
    And roads where fools will try
To say farewell with kisses;
    Touch love and say good-bye.

We met on roads of laughter,
    Now wistful roads depart,
For I must hurry after
    To overtake my heart.

Clasped Hands

Rose M. Fink

My hands have known the gentle touch
Of many soft and wondrous things:
The velvet of a beagle's ear,
The magic of a pigeon's wings,
A baby's dimpled, curving cheek —
Just newly washed and newly come —
The gossamer of milkweed silk,
The nuzzle of a lamb, new-born.
For these, dear Lord, I thank Thee much,
For this, dear Lord, I thank Thee more:
Our hands entwined while life shall last —
His hand on ours forevermore!

A SLICE OF LIFE

— Edgar A. Guest —

Gift-Bearing Man

A box of candy under his arm
    Adds to a man a touch of charm.
A smile of welcome he's sure to win
    Who, carrying sweets, comes walking in.
And this is well-known in the candy shops:
    Many flaws are hidden with chocolate drops.

Candy and flowers and a trinket small
    Improve the lover who comes to call.
He may be ugly, but there and then
    The maiden will think him the best of men;
And his faults, however so grim they be,
    Until after marriage she'll never see.

Well, the years are long and our traits grow plain,
    But candy and flowers great aids remain.
And a man will be loved when his worst is known
    If by little gifts often his best is shown.
All grandpas know, until life takes wing,
    They are watched for and loved for the sweets they bring.

Edgar A. Guest began his illustrious career in 1895 at the age of fourteen when his work first appeared in the Detroit Free Press. His column was syndicated in over 300 newspapers, and he became known as "The Poet of the People."

THROUGH MY WINDOW

Pamela Kennedy

Art by Russ Flint

LOVE GIFTS

A few weeks ago I got together with some friends and the subject of Valentine's Day came up. As we chatted, one woman asked, "What was the best love gift you ever received?" The hostess got up, walked out of the room, and returned with a little box. She placed it on the coffee table and smiled.

"That," she announced, "is mine."

The box was about four inches long, two inches high, and two inches wide. It was covered with elbow macaroni spray-painted gold and embellished with faux pearls. We all looked at it, but no one said anything. It was clearly one of those situations where beauty was in the eye of the beholder. Laughing, my friend picked it up, opened the hinged lid, and took out a piece of paper.

"This is a box of love. Whenever you need some, just open the lid and breathe in deeply. There will always be plenty, because it is from me. Love, Cindy." She took a deep breath and closed the box, placing it back on the table. "When Cindy was in third grade, she made this for me in Girl Scouts. It was touching and cute then, but I never realized how much it would mean now that she is married and living across the country."

"Pass the tissues!" pleaded a misty-eyed friend as we sat gazing at the gilded macaroni. "That's the sweetest thing I ever heard." There were nods of agreement and then another woman spoke up.

"My husband and I were given a wonderful love gift a few years ago by some creative friends. Our kids were six, four, and two, and we were living on a shoestring, emotionally and financially. Susan and Ben invited us over to dinner on a Friday night. When we got to their house, however, there was a note on the door telling us just to come on in. We found a beautifully set table with crystal, silver, candles, and flowers, but no host or hostess. Then we discovered a letter on the table. Susan and Ben informed us they were giving us a romantic night out at their house while they watched our kids at ours! They had prepared a delicious dinner for us, had put romantic music on the stereo, and had even decorated the guest bedroom with flowers and chocolates on the pillows! It was the most thoughtful and loving thing anyone has ever done for us."

There was general agreement that Susan and Ben deserved a Nobel Prize for love.

"My love gift wasn't nearly so extravagant," interjected another friend, "but it sure meant a lot to me." She went on to relate how she and her husband had grown apart over the years and how, at one point, they had reached a place where it seemed love had died. She decided to take a trip to be alone and think about their relationship. Upon arriving at her destination, she opened her suitcase and found an envelope tucked in her clothing. As she opened it, out fell a photograph taken of the two of them at their wedding reception. On the back her husband had penned, "Remember? I love you. Let's start over." She never finished unpacking. "It was the beginning of a wonderful reconciliation; a real turning point in our relationship. Look." She pulled out her purse and passed around the shopworn photograph.

We all handled it with a certain reverence, as we examined the young bride and groom and read the heartfelt message on the back, awed at the power of love so simply and honestly expressed.

We went around the circle then, each one sharing some love gift given by a friend or family member, and it was a delightful and uplifting afternoon. It was good to recall the ways we had been loved by others. But the realization I came away with was the fact that love need not be limited to a certain holiday or even to traditional ways of expression. The gifts that most touched us were those given by people who saw a place of need and freely filled the void. They were gifts given with an extravagance of the heart, not necessarily of the pocketbook. I was reminded of the apostle Paul's words as he wrote to his little flock in Corinth centuries ago: "Love is patient, love is kind. It does not envy, it does not boast, it is not proud. It always protects, always trusts, always hopes, always perseveres." On Valentine's Day and every day, these are the love gifts that matter most.

Pamela Kennedy is a freelance writer of short stories, articles, essays, and children's books. Wife of a naval officer and mother of three children, she has made her home on both U.S. coasts and currently resides in Honolulu, Hawaii. She draws her material from her own experiences and memories, adding highlights from her imagination to add to the story.

Mother's Valentine

Lucille King

My mother made a valentine
    So very long ago
And decked it out all prettily,
    Like for a special beau.

I watched her as she cut the heart
    Then frilled it up with lace
And worked artistically away,
    A smile upon her face.

She wove a ribbon, shiny red,
    Among the lace so white

Then placed a picture of herself
    Through a slit she cut inside.

I saw the words, "I love you, Dear,
    I'm proud to be your wife.
You've given me the blessings
    Of a blissful, wedded life."

I felt like laughing out for joy;
    My childish heart was glad!
Mom's special valentine would go
    To a special beau named Dad.

LOVE FROM TWO VALENTINES
Dianne Dietrich Leis Photography

My Valentine

Nona Ferrel

My favorite valentine is not
A frilly one with lace
And bows and fancy trimmings
I can buy most any place.

The one I like is crudely wrought
And somewhat smudged, with wobbly lines.
Each word endeared with passing years
"To Mother. Be my valentine."

Best Valentine

Alice B. Johnson

No valentine can take the place
Or, through a lifetime's span, erase
The memoried one that always lingers,
Made by small and fumbling fingers.

Puckered brow and bitten lip,
Fearful of a scissor's snip;
A crooked heart, unsteady arrow,
Letters like the tracks of sparrows;

Symbol of a child's emotion,
Written with heartfelt devotion.
"I love you so, dear Mom of mine,
Will you be my valentine?"

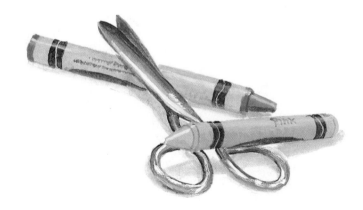

Stolen Heart

Reginald Holmes

The darling of the neighborhood,
   This captivating blonde;
And she has stolen every heart
   For many blocks beyond.

Her smile is like an angel's smile,
   Her eyes are violet-blue;
Her golden hair is like the gleam
   Of sunlight shining through.

There isn't a man in all the world
   Who can resist her charms;
Or one who can conceal a wish
   To hold her in his arms.

The day she came into my life
   Is one I won't forget;
I knew that she was meant for me
   The instant that we met.

With just a look, I knew that she
   Was meant to hug and hold;
And she is still my valentine
   Although she's two years old!

SNOWY SWEETHEART
Caroline Wood
F-Stock Photo Agency

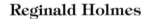

A Valentine Prayer

Gertrude Rudberg

O Lord, I ask before I start,
As Valentine's comes round,
That I may find within my heart
Its meaning deep, profound.

I ask Thee, Lord, that I may find
Some place where there is need,
Where I can be a little kind
And plant a friendly seed.

I ask Thee, Lord, that I might give
A little bit of love
To those I've felt I can't forgive
As Thou dost from above.

I ask Thee, Lord, to be my guide,
Grant patience, courage too
That I may e'er with Thee abide
In all I try to do.

FOR THE CHILDREN
ARTWORK BY RUSS FLINT

THE SNOWBIRD
Hezekiah Butterworth

In the rosy light trills the gay swallow,
The thrush, in the roses below;
The meadowlark sings in the meadow,
But the snowbird sings in the snow.
    Ah me!
    Chickadee!
The snowbird sings in the snow.

The blue martin trills in the gable,
The wren, in the gourd below;
In the elm flutes the golden robin,
But the snowbird sings in the snow.
    Ah me!
    Chickadee!
The snowbird sings in the snow.

I love the high heart of the osprey,
The meek heart of the thrush below,
The heart of the lark in the meadow,
And the snowbird's heart in the snow.
    But dearest to me,
    Chickadee! Chickadee!
Is that true little heart in the snow.

*The unique perspective of Russ Flint's artistic style
has made him a favorite of* Ideals *readers for many
years. A resident of California and father of four,
Russ Flint has illustrated a children's Bible and
many other books.*

Skating Party

Florence S. Reed

A picture of the old mill pond
Recalls the afternoons we donned
Our warmest skating togs when school
Was done and hiked to the frozen pool.

Played crack-the-whip, cut figure eights;
Ice crackled to the whir of skates.
The horse-drawn bobsled filled with hay
Awaited us not far away.

But all too soon the sun dropped low
To warn us it was time to go.
In memory nothing can compare
With skating fun in frosty air.

Readers' Reflections

Winter Storm

Inside my window snug and warm,
I watch the chilling winter storm.
First freezing rain as slick as glass
Coats tree and bush and blades of grass.
Then falls the snow in blanket white
That covers everything in sight.
Like feathery blossoms floating down,
The fluffy snowflakes grace the town.
As through the yard the soft snow swirls

In mounds and peaks and drifts, it swirls.
The wind sweeps snow before my door.
And I am thankful evermore,
That I am safe and snug and warm
Protected from the chilling storm.

Mary I. Widney
Watonga, Oklahoma

Winter Song

Winter is upon us,
    And everyone you meet
Resembles frosty snowmen
    Rushing past on booted feet.

Winter is upon us,
    Yet only children cheer;
For only they among us
    See the season quite so clear;

Note the taste of snowflakes,
    As caviar quite fine;

Lick crystal sticks of ice
    Like connoisseurs of wine;

Consider that their sitting part
    Most amply fills the bill
To skidder over icy creeks,
    To plummet down a hill.

Oh, bless their childhood vision,
    Their innocence and zest,
For choosing out of all the year
    To love the winter best.

Bea-Ellen Bollinger Lotz
Wellington, Ontario

Winter Cathedral

As I walk through the quiet solitude
Of a wintry forest
I stand in awe of the mighty oaks,
Whose branches are cloaked in robes of frosty white.

A symbol of God's great strength
As they reach forever upward
Toward the heavens.

Calmness pervades earth's grandest cathedral
Where the elements are interwoven
By the Master's hand.

Nature is at peace
While animals roam the trails
Of a patchwork of autumn's moist, fallen leaves.
The calling of a bird rends the silence
As my thoughts run deep.

Softly I whisper
As I linger still,
"I trespass here,
For this is Thine."

Then, seemingly from the hills all 'round,
I hear the reply,
"Oh, but my son,
I have created it for thee."

Larry Lamb
Quincy, Illinois

Snow Message

Snow falls gently
    Through the night
And clothes the world
    In linen white.

When we awake
    And see it so
We feel renewed,
    Our souls aglow.

A promise here
    Is in the air
Of what God plans
    For us to share.

This bright snow world,
    Soft and yielding,
Speaks of peace
    And joy unending.

Gene Ash
Lancaster, Ohio

Editor's Note: Readers are invited to submit unpublished, original poetry for possible publication in future issues of Ideals. *Please send copies only; manuscripts will not be returned. Writers receive $10 for each published submission. Send material to "Readers' Reflections," Ideals Publications Inc., P.O. Box 148000, Nashville, TN 37214-8000.*

Country Winter

Lon Myruski

I recall the country pleasures
Of my childhood on the farm;
Where life was plain and simple,
Yet steeped in country charm.
I hold each season's mem'ries
Clasped sweetly 'neath my breast,
But those of country winter
Are ones I cherish best.

How the sun rose o'er our valley
Like a frosty tangerine,
Dripping on the snowdrifts
Turned fiery velveteen.
And the snow-clad barbed wire fences
Stretched down long winding lanes,
Embracing country winter
In rows like velvet chains.

There were times just after snowfall
When the world was without sound;
The slate gray sky in silence,
The mute marshmallow ground.
Then somewhere from the distance
Came snowbird serenades—
Their songs of country winter
In joyous accolades.

On some nights I'd lie and listen
To the cold wind's whistling tune,
While cuddled 'neath my patch quilt
As clouds caressed the moon.
Then I'd get the warmest feeling
And drift the night away
In dreams of country winter,
As I still do today.

Country CHRONICLE

Lansing Christman

Dear and caring friends always remember me with valentines. They not only give me comfort and hope, they cheer me and lift my spirits to brighter horizons.

This year I have a new valentine, a schoolgirl living miles from me, a girl I have never met and probably never will. I call her my valentine, though I am sure she knows nothing about me.

I am a member of The Nature Conservancy, and the little girl's message was included in material that came from that organization which devotes all its energies to the preservation of our environment.

The schoolgirl's letter reveals that she is looking centuries ahead to assure that the planet will still exist. She wrote: "Dear Mr. or Ms. of The Nature Conservancy. My name is Petra Michelle Sander, and I would like to know what I should do to help our planet make it past the twenty-fifth century. No matter how horrid life is by then, I would like to assure that there is still life. Make Earth Day every day. Petra."

The Nature Conservancy said: "Isn't that wonderful? Especially coming from a grade-schooler! Here we are trying to chart a course for the next decade, and up there in Amherst, Massachusetts, is a young schoolgirl thinking about life on earth 800 years from now."

It is up to us to help Petra Michelle Sander fulfill her dreams. Her dreams and aspirations have made her one of my valentines. It does not matter that she and I don't even know one another. From this moment on I shall consider Petra Michelle Sander one of my cherished valentines. This from a man in his eighties in the foothills of the Blue Ridge Mountains to a little girl with her dreams way up there in Amherst, Massachusetts.

This is my valentine to her. She writes from the heart and so do I.

The author of two published books, Lansing Christman has been contributing to Ideals *for over twenty years. Mr. Christman has also been published in several American, foreign, and braille anthologies. He lives in rural South Carolina.*

YOUNG PONDEROSA PINES
Deschutes National Forest, Oregon
Jeff Gnass Photography

To February

Essie L. Mariner

There is no lovelier sight I know
Than trees and hedges clothed in snow;
Their branches wreathed in flowers of white
Makes fairy daytime of the night.

When the moon's bright silver glow
Shines o'er a far expanse of snow,
I stand in awe, for rustic things
Stand here and there in angel's wings.

I love to have you come to me,
Clothing each house, each fence, each tree.
There is no lovelier sight I know
Than all the world when clothed in snow.

FROSTED COTTONWOODS AND PINES
Indian Valley, Sierra Nevada, California
Jeff Gnass Photography

Jewels

Mamie Ozburn Odom

The snow falls soft and gently clings,
Pure and fragile as fairies' wings.
An ermine coat covers the sod
Like little stars sent down by God;
Each one a jewel, a polished gem;
They crown the earth a diadem.

The windowpanes have pictures etched
In filigree the North wind fetched.
And on the hearth, brown chestnuts toast
As sweet potatoes slowly roast,
And popping corn is snowy white
And making candy is a delight.

We laugh in glee; the snow falls light—
White snow sent down for just tonight.
We feel as rich as royalty,
Snug and happy as can be;
But day will come and to our sorrow
The sun will melt our gems tomorrow.

WEDDING CAKE HOUSE
Kennebunk, Maine
Gene Ahrens Photography

Frosted Windows

Minnie Klemme

The windows in my little house
Are very bright tonight,
With fragile ferns and fronded palms,
So delicate and white.

How skillfully the frost pursues
An old and honored art.
It may not last the season,
But it's etched upon my heart.

When the summer flowers fade and die
And the autumn trees are bare,
I look to my window
And the artistry that's there.

TWIN SURPRISE. Superstock, Inc.

Raining Cats & Dogs

Maryann Hammers

*P*ulling off desolate State Highway 1 on a cold, damp January evening, my husband, José, and I found ourselves in a tiny northern California town. After checking in at a motel just off the highway, we walked along the town's short main street in search of a hot meal. We would get a good night's rest, we said, and rise early in the morning to tour the redwood forest.

As we sloshed our way down the wet sidewalk, José suddenly whistled and kissed the air. "Hi, boy," he called. The night was so dark I hadn't even seen the black dog on the side of the road. It jumped up and appreciatively sniffed and licked at José's offered hand.

"Poor guy!" I said. "He's soaked." It had rained on and off all day, and the dog was drenched, bedraggled, and scruffy.

We murmured sympathetically for the dog's plight and continued on our way. The dog followed. We crossed the street. The dog crossed the street. We turned around. The dog turned around. We sighed. The dog wagged his tail eagerly.

A few minutes later we stood in a supermarket parking lot, popping open a tall can of dog food, which our new friend sucked up in one breath. "Wow," I said and returned to the store for another can. Whoosh! Gone. The dog looked at us expectantly.

We bought three more cans, along with a big bag of dry food that I poured on the ground in hefty piles. Three cashiers joined us in the parking lot.

"Oh, poor doggie."

"I wish I could take him."

"He's starving! And so wet!"

Everyone sympathized, but no one could help. One checker, however, thought that a woman who served breakfast at a local diner sometimes took in lost pets.

We walked the two blocks or so back to our room. The dog obediently trotted at our heels, stopping only once to sniff a greeting to a beautiful German shepherd that sat regally in front of a video store.

"Oh, no," my husband groaned, and I looked behind us.

And then there were two.

No one in the video store—which, along with

the coffee shop, was the only establishment open—had ever seen either dog before.

When we returned to our room, I poured dry food in the plastic ice bucket and placed it on the porch in case the dogs got hungry. At the rattle of the food in the bowl, as if on cue, a wiry, tiger-striped kitten darted from nowhere into our room. She hungrily buried her face in the bag of dog food.

Disbelieving, my husband shouted, "No! Get rid of the cat!"

"I can't!" I wailed. And I couldn't. How could I? Contentedly licking her paws and loudly purring her thanks, this cat wasn't going anywhere. I hadn't the heart to throw her into the cold night, especially with those two big dogs sitting on the welcome mat. José too lost his bravado when the cat jumped on his lap and, affectionately kneading her paws and batting her head against his chest, settled comfortably.

And then there were three.

Since we still hadn't eaten, we decided to figure out a solution to our animal situation after dinner. Half an hour later, we glumly faced each other over meat loaf and mashed potatoes and gravy. Two dogs, with a plastic ice bucket of kibble, waited for us at the motel. In case the kitten, who relaxed inside, should get the late-night munchies, we left her one ashtray filled with dog food, another with water. José was worried that the motel manager would kick us out for so flagrantly disobeying the no pets rule.

"Now what?" we asked each other. Here we were, vacationing hundreds of miles from our tiny, yardless Los Angeles condominium, and we were suddenly responsible for two homeless but very nice dogs and one cat.

We decided to wait till morning; then we would track down the animal woman in the diner and take it from there. As we drowned our worries in apple pie and ice cream, my husband glanced out the window.

"Look!" he said and pointed to a man walking a poodle across the street. Trotting behind them was our black dog! The three turned a corner and disappeared.

"Well, that's one less dog to worry about," José said. But I felt strangely betrayed. What ungracious lack of appreciation, what callous abandonment!

When we returned to our room, the loyal German shepherd was on the porch, patiently awaiting us, and the cat was curled up on the bed, where she spent the night.

The next morning, we planned to deal with the animals, then check out of the motel and proceed on our trip. When I opened the door to load the car, the cat raced outside, heading for the dense forest surrounding the town. "Kitty cat!" I shouted, but she ignored my calls. In no time, she was out of sight.

And then there was one.

The German shepherd and I walked to the diner where the grocery clerk had suggested I might find the woman who helps strays. I opened my mouth to inquire when a man at the counter stepped in front of me.

"Queenie, where the heck have you been?" he said, scolding the dog. "I looked for you all night!"

Feeling unburdened and free, I returned to finish packing. We could hit the road and enjoy the rest of our vacation. I hummed my way back to the motel.

But when I returned to our room, there was the cat, stretched out under the blue plastic chair. She purred and licked her paws as though she lived there. I stared in dismay.

"Oh, you met our cat," a voice behind me said. It was the hotel manager. "The cat lives here," she continued. "We get lots of fishermen staying here, and the cat begs for scraps. Nice cat." She smiled.

An hour later, we were driving through spectacular redwood forests along the Avenue of the Giants in the Humbolt Redwoods State Park. Mist and fog and sun filtered through the trees. It couldn't have been more beautiful. I sat in the car, mourning.

The camera swung from José's neck as he returned from capturing a gorgeous shot of fog and sunlight patches. "What's wrong?" he asked.

"I miss my pets!" I wailed.

The Letter

Beatrice M. Murphy

Please excuse this letter;
I know we said we're through,
But there's something very precious
Of mine you took with you
And I must have it back.

I'm sure that you will find it
If you search among your pack,
Way down in the innermost part.

Please wrap it carefully
Before you mail—
You see, it is my heart.

Photo Above
ROSEBUD
Bruce Curtis Photography

Opposite Page
CORRESPONDENCE
Pellegrini
International Stock Photo

TRAVELER'S *Diary*

Lisa C. Thompson

VICTORIAN HOMES IN ALAMO SQUARE. San Francisco, California. James Blank, FPG International.

PAINTED LADIES OF SAN FRANCISCO
Victorian Architecture in San Francisco, California

Not long ago, a view of the city of San Francisco provided a striking white vista. White on white houses gleamed against the blue bay beyond and the blue sky above. The late 1960s saw the birth of the Colorist Movement, which inspired homeowners throughout the city to renovate their charming Victorians and repaint them in their original colors. Enthusiastic preservationists joined the colorists and soon homeowners began experimenting with color in bold, creative ways. Real estate developers saw the potential buried within these faded old homes and halted the eager bulldozers. Neighborhoods across the city came alive with the colorful transformation of these Victorian homes that came to be called "Painted Ladies." Today, a view of San Francisco more closely resembles a Cézanne painting with its rich variety of vibrant colors blending and contrasting on a blue canvas.

The Painted Ladies of San Francisco were constructed during the prosperous gold mining frenzy of the mid- to late-1800s, which brought settlers to the San Francisco Bay area by the thousands. Eager to show off their new-found wealth, these pioneers demanded showy homes with elaborate ornamentation. Builders added lacy gingerbread millwork, Corinthian columns, plaster garlands, gabled rooftops, and even turrets to please their fussy customers. And color! The old standby colors of Colonial Revival white and Navy gray simply would not do. Settlers wanted bright, contrasting yet coordinating colors to celebrate their affluence.

One of the most popular styles of Victorian architecture in nineteenth century San Francisco was the San Francisco stick style. The stick style is so-named for the strips of wood that outline the exterior of the house, windows, and doorways. These strips were painted in bright colors that accented the vibrant color of the house.

The interiors of the Painted Ladies were just as fussy as the exteriors. Displaying family photographs, personal memorabilia, and travel souvenirs—all examples of personal wealth—was of utmost importance to the Victorian family. Interior decor frequently included plush carpets in vivid colors on glowing wood floors, richly patterned wallpapers, lace curtains,

VICTORIAN BEAUTY. San Francisco, California.
Dennis Hallinan, FPG International.

chandeliers, and ornate furniture. The front parlor was in particular a highly decorated room. As the most important room in the house, it had to be perfect, since the household's most important guests were entertained there. The family's best furniture, carpets, trinkets, etc., were displayed in the front parlor with pride.

Nearly 50,000 elaborate Victorian homes were built before 1906 in the San Francisco Bay area, but little more than 13,000 survive today. Those that have survived, however, have been lovingly restored by their owners to bring back the charm of yesteryear. Today's Painted Ladies were created in one of two ways. Some homeowners chose to determine the original colors of their homes and then used today's paints and materials to match those colors as closely as possible. Other homeowners simply chose colors that were historically correct for the type of home they owned and in shades that would effectively bring out the hidden delights of its intricate details.

Victorian architecture can be found all over San Francisco, but the following neighborhoods have some outstanding examples of Painted Ladies: Alamo Square, Eureka Valley, Noe Valley, Pacific Heights, Haight Ashbury, the Mission District, and downtown. Several tours are offered, and some even include viewing the interior of these lovely homes. Since several of the Painted Ladies have been transformed into Bed-and-Breakfast establishments, you could even spend the night in San Francisco surrounded by old-fashioned Victorian elegance.

On Monsieur's Departure

Queen Elizabeth I

I grieve and dare not show my discontent.
I love and yet am forced to seem to hate.
I do, yet dare not say I ever meant.
I seem stark mute but inwardly do prate.
   I am and not, I freeze and yet am burned,
   Since from myself another self I turned.

My care is like my shadow in the sun—
Follows me flying, flies when I pursue it,
Stands and lies by me, doth what I have done.
His too familiar care doth make me rue it.
   No means I find to rid him from my breast,
   Till by the end of things it be suppressed.

Some gentler passion slide into my mind,
For I am soft and made of melting snow;
Or be more cruel, love, and so be kind,
Let me float or sink, be high or low.
   Or let me live with some more sweet content
   Or die and so forget what love ere meant.

60

TREASURES OF TIME
Superstock Inc.

MEET MR. LINCOLN

D id Mr. Lincoln look like that?" Well, that all depends. To this question, so frequently asked both now and in Lincoln's lifetime, artists have given many different answers. As a consequence, the face of Abraham Lincoln has been made familiar to people all over the world and the man himself has become accepted as the most distinguished and representative American.

Such was not always the case. When Lincoln was nominated as the Republican candidate for the Presidency of the United States, the American people generally had so little knowledge of his life and appearance that it was necessary to prepare hastily a number of campaign "lives" and portraits of the candidate. Writers and artists hastened to Springfield to be received cordially by an extremely busy man who could give them but little of his time.

The artists set up shop in the Governor's Room in the Old State House, which had been assigned for Lincoln's use during the campaign, and worked upon their portraits while Lincoln was attending to his correspondence, swapping stories with old friends, or receiving distinguished visitors. These likenesses were supplemented by lithographs and engravings of "sun pictures"—as Mr. Lincoln called photographs—taken to meet increasing demand. Today we possess so many of them that another portrait, more or less, is hardly news. Many of these portraits, however, were painted after Lincoln's passing, and for the most part by artists who had never seen him in life.

A new contemporary likeness is, therefore, always a matter of real importance. Especially is this true when, as in the case of the "beardless" portrait of Mr. Lincoln by George Peter Alexander Healy, the artist produces a fresh and striking interpretation of the man who was destined to lead this nation through its darkest days. It is now hanging in the Corcoran Gallery of Art in Washington, D.C.

Mr. Healy was an American artist of distinction. He was born in Boston and did much of his early work in his native city. The exact number of Healy's portraits is not known, but it seems that he neglected no person of note.

Healy is known to have painted at one sitting a small portrait of President Lincoln at the White House in May 1861 following the artist's return to the North from Charleston, where he had witnessed the attack on Fort Sumter. He made another study shortly after the assassination, which was used later in the large historical painting entitled "The Peacemakers." The original of this study is probably the one owned by the Newberry Library in Chicago. A copy of it (painted by Healy) hangs in the state dining room at the White House. It was presented to the nation by the heirs of Robert T. Lincoln. Another copy, also by the artist, was purchased by Andrew W. Mellon and was included in his original gift to the National Gallery of Art.

In his *Reminiscences* Mr. Healy makes several references to the fact that Mr. Lincoln sat for him for a portrait or portraits. The facts as he gives them are not too clear and they have been made more obscure by confusion as to when and where these sittings took place. It is now certain that Lincoln sat for Healy in Springfield in the autumn of 1860, and in Washington in May, 1861. The statements in Healy's autobiography have not been associated with either of these occasions, but have been distorted to refer to the "bearded" portrait which was painted in Chicago in 1866 or 1867.

The earliest of the Healy portraits of Lincoln has long been in the possession of the Corcoran Gallery of Art and has only recently emerged from its obscurity. It was purchased on April 26, 1879, along with sixteen other portraits by the same artist, from Thomas Barbour Bryan, formerly of Chicago, but at the time a resident of Washington. Mr. Bryan was a close friend and patron of the artist, and an ardent admirer of Mr. Lincoln. The records of the Gallery state that this portrait "was painted expressly for Mr. Bryan." Nothing has yet been discovered to confirm the statement. The painting appears in the catalogue of the permanent collection of the Gallery and is listed elsewhere among the more important of Mr. Healy's works.

In his *Reminiscences* Healy mentions that during a sitting Mr. Lincoln showed him a letter from a lady who suggested that he should grow a beard to hide his "horrible lantern jaws." But he is mistaken when he suggests that this was in Springfield after he left the city in February 1861.

Robert Todd Lincoln confirms the artist at one point and corrects him at another. In a letter to Richard Watson Gilder, dated February 24, 1908, the son of the martyred President says: "Mr. Healy painted a small portrait of my father about the time of his first election. There is nothing remarkable about it." The "whisker" episode refers of course to the letter Mr. Lincoln received from Grace Bedell— a small girl—of Westfield, New York, to which he replied on October 19, 1860. Shortly thereafter Mr. Lincoln decided to grow a beard.

The argument is clinched by three other bits of evidence. The first is a letter written by Thomas Webster, Jr., to John Sherman on November 15, 1860. The letter is now in the Library of Congress and in it the writer describes to Mr. Sherman his visit to Mr. Lincoln "when he sat for Mr. Healy, the

Healy. ABRAHAM LINCOLN, 1860. Oil on canvas, 30 ⅜ x 25 ⅜ in (77.15 x 64.45 cm). In the Collection of the Corcoran Gallery of Art, Museum Purchase, Gallery Fund.

famous portrait painter." The second consists of items from the *Illinois State Journal* of October 26, November 1 and 14, 1860, which state that Hesse Atwood, a Philadelphia artist, "is in Springfield painting two portraits of Mr. Lincoln." These depict Lincoln wearing a beard. The third is from the *Chicago Tribune* of November 17, 1860, which announces that "Healy's portrait of Lincoln is on exhibit at his studio, No. 333 Lake Street. It is the best that has been taken of our next President."

This review of the facts authenticates the painting and adds another document to aid us in our understanding of the great, good, and patient man. But when was it painted?

There is no doubt that it could not have been painted before Lincoln received the letter from Grace Bedell, nor after the painting by Jesse Atwood, which is the first to show the President-elect with a beard. Healy was undoubtedly at work upon it during the third week of October, 1860, and most surely had completed it, save for retouching, before November 1 of that year.

How the picture came into Mr. Bryan's possession has not been determined. He probably purchased it, just as he did later the copy of the Emancipation Proclamation which was sold at the great Sanitary Fair in Chicago. At any rate, here is Mr. Healy's earliest interpretation of Mr. Lincoln's personality. When compared with his later work, many will regard this first likeness as his best portrayal of a complex and profound character. You will like Mr. Lincoln!

Originally printed in The Christian Science Monitor Magazine, *February 10, 1945.*

The Miracle Heart

Lois J. Funk

The label read "Fragile. Handle with love.
Contents: One Miracle Heart from Above.
If personalization of heart is desired,
Just follow these steps. (Some assembly required.)"

Step one said, "Take your love plus My love for you
And fill up the heart, then proceed to step two."
So I gathered some love that I knew was from Him
And, with most of my love, filled the heart to the brim;
Holding back just a little in case of a spill,
Being careful to keep the heart quiet and still.

Step two said, "If love doesn't flow from the heart,
Then the heart did not open; go back to the start.
And just to make certain step one is complete:
When the love starts to flow, then you'll hear the heart beat.
But if, after all, love still fails to flow,
Then check, step by step, 'Troubleshooting,' below."

Well, of course, I knew better. I chiseled and tried
To pry open the heart with the love locked inside,
But love just wasn't flowing, with all that I'd done,
So I stubbornly turned back to step number one.
Over and over I read it again,
But before I gave up, I finally gave in.
When I checked "Troubleshooting" to see what was wrong,
I found the instructions were right all along.

For it read, "You must follow step one to a 'T',
Using ALL of your love plus that given by Me.
So don't hold any back, and if any should spill,
Let it flow out to others who still need their fill.
Just make sure that you follow this step every day,
For your love cannot grow till you give it away;
But the heart isn't yours till the love in it grows,
And no miracle comes till the heart overflows."

So I refilled the heart till its love overflowed,
Till it beat with a rhythm that couldn't be slowed,
And then, in the fine print, read "Let it be known
That this Miracle Heart is now truly your own."

64

ROSES OF LOVE
Bruce Curtis Photography

Ideals' *Family Recipes*

Favorite Recipes from the Ideals Family of Readers

Editor's Note: Please send us your best-loved recipes! Mail a typed copy of the recipe along with your name, address, and telephone number to Ideals *magazine, ATTN: Recipes, P.O. Box 148000, Nashville, Tennessee 37214-8000. We will pay $10 for each recipe used. Recipes cannot be returned.*

TEATIME TASSIES

In a mixing bowl, cream one 3-ounce package cream cheese with ½ cup margarine. Gradually blend in 1 cup flour. Chill at least 1 hour.

In a separate bowl, cream 1 tablespoon softened margarine with ¾ cup brown sugar, packed. Stir in 1 egg, dash salt, and 1 teaspoon vanilla. Set aside.

Roll chilled cream cheese mixture into 1-inch balls. Place balls in tiny muffin tins and press on bottom and sides of tins. Sprinkle ½ cup chopped pecans in each muffin. Top with brown sugar mixture, then another ½ cup chopped pecans. Bake in a preheated 325° oven until filling is set, approximately 20 to 25 minutes. Makes 24.

Esther Willard
Glastonbury, Connecticut

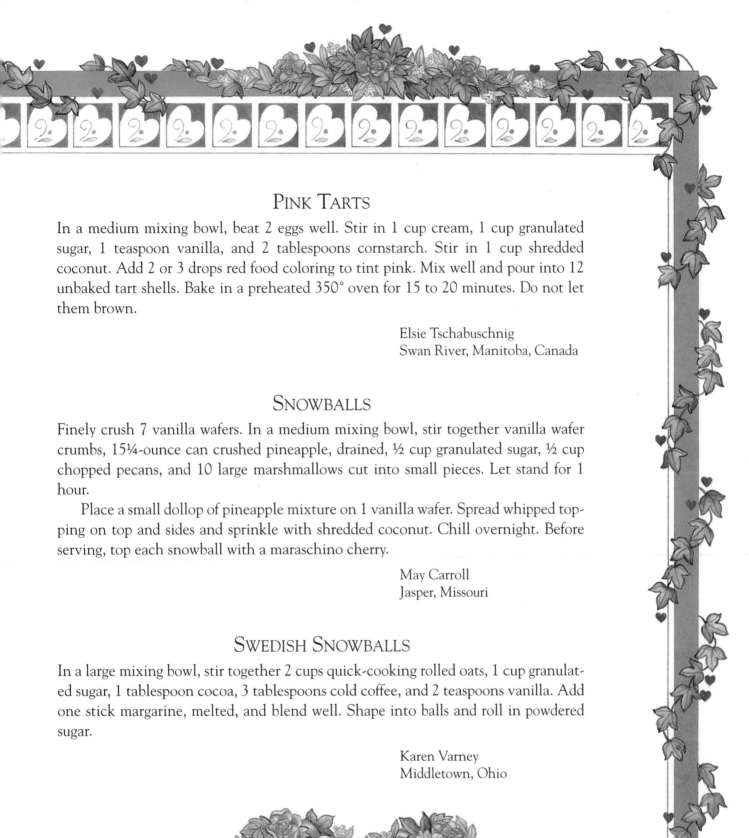

PINK TARTS

In a medium mixing bowl, beat 2 eggs well. Stir in 1 cup cream, 1 cup granulated sugar, 1 teaspoon vanilla, and 2 tablespoons cornstarch. Stir in 1 cup shredded coconut. Add 2 or 3 drops red food coloring to tint pink. Mix well and pour into 12 unbaked tart shells. Bake in a preheated 350° oven for 15 to 20 minutes. Do not let them brown.

Elsie Tschabuschnig
Swan River, Manitoba, Canada

SNOWBALLS

Finely crush 7 vanilla wafers. In a medium mixing bowl, stir together vanilla wafer crumbs, 15¼-ounce can crushed pineapple, drained, ½ cup granulated sugar, ½ cup chopped pecans, and 10 large marshmallows cut into small pieces. Let stand for 1 hour.

Place a small dollop of pineapple mixture on 1 vanilla wafer. Spread whipped topping on top and sides and sprinkle with shredded coconut. Chill overnight. Before serving, top each snowball with a maraschino cherry.

May Carroll
Jasper, Missouri

SWEDISH SNOWBALLS

In a large mixing bowl, stir together 2 cups quick-cooking rolled oats, 1 cup granulated sugar, 1 tablespoon cocoa, 3 tablespoons cold coffee, and 2 teaspoons vanilla. Add one stick margarine, melted, and blend well. Shape into balls and roll in powdered sugar.

Karen Varney
Middletown, Ohio

Nancy Skarmeas

Edith Wharton
Writer

Edith Wharton was born and raised in a society where social functions, home decor, entertaining, and travel occupied the thoughts and energy of most women, a world where art and literature were regarded with distrust or, at the least, disinterest. Nonetheless, Wharton was to become one of the most prolific of American novelists, taking as her subject matter the very society that dismissed and often disapproved of her art. In the comfortable but stifling environment of late nineteenth-century New York City society, Edith Wharton found the inspiration for a body of writing that has earned a permanent place in the American literary canon and that has preserved a portrait of a unique and fascinating era in American history.

Edith Wharton was born Edith Newbold Jones in January of 1862. She was the youngest child and only daughter of a considerably wealthy family with a well-established place in the fashionable New York society. The Joneses spent winters in their

New York City brownstone and summers in Newport, Rhode Island; a routine broken only by regular trips to Europe with groups of friends, where they saw the sights of the great cities but kept their insular New York social circle intact. The Joneses and their contemporaries valued their traditions and their rules for behavior. Theirs was a world that demanded conformity and that offered little encouragement to a young girl with an active, intelligent mind.

Edith Jones, however, showed early signs of just such a mind. On an extended family trip to Europe between the ages of three and nine, she learned to speak German, Italian, and French as her family moved from country to country. As a teenager, she wrote and had privately published a volume of poetry—this despite the disapproval of family and friends, who believed that such pursuits were below the standards of a girl of her class. The Joneses' hopes for their daughter included a basic education, a successful society debut, marriage, and a place at the head of her own fashionable household; writing poetry was not part of the picture. And, despite her precociousness, young Edith was not a rebellious child. She played the role of society daughter with precision and flair. She made her debut at seventeen, married a wealthy Boston banker at twenty-three, set up homes in New York, Newport, and later, in the Berkshires of Massachusetts, and traveled each February to Europe. In short, Edith Jones Wharton appeared to be the picture of conformity.

Still, the love of writing that she had discovered as a teenager remained. After settling into the routine of her married life, Edith Wharton again sought expression through writing, this time with a series of short stories and verses published in *Scribner's* and *Harper's* magazines. This success led to her coauthorship of a book on interior decorating, which made a great splash with a call for a return to more conservative and classical values in home decor. Wharton's first novel appeared not long after; in 1902, Edith Wharton, forty years old, published *The Valley of Decision*, which effectively launched her career as a full-time author. For the next thirty-five years, Wharton produced more than a book a year. By her death in 1937, she had written close to fifty novels.

For all of her life Edith Wharton had, on the surface, followed to perfection the path laid out for her at birth—social functions, travel, good taste, and good manners. Beneath that surface, however, she had quietly nurtured her intellect and her creativity. In the novels she wrote during her forties and fifties, her two worlds came together as she created art out of the artless, insular world of the New York social scene. Her first critical and popular success was *The House of Mirth*. Through the experiences of the heroine, Lily Bart, this novel tells the story of the clash of two worlds—the old New York of the Joneses and the more modern city of "new money" and new values that began to emerge with the great oil and steel fortunes of the late-nineteenth century. Wharton's portrait of young Lily, caught between two conflicting worlds with tragic results, is authentic and moving. In a later novel, *The Age of Innocence*, Wharton looked back more fondly on the world of her youth, perhaps because with the coming of the twentieth century and World War I, it had been destroyed forever. *The Age of Innocence* is a story of the redemptive power of love. It won the Pulitzer Prize and is still treasured today for its colorful, painstakingly detailed portrayal of the life and style of the brownstones of New York and the mansions of Newport in the 1870s. These two novels typify the admirable work of Edith Wharton—sometimes lovingly nostalgic, sometimes harshly critical, her writing paints a vibrant portrait of the world she knew best.

Many readers today know Edith Wharton more for her novel *Ethan Frome*—set in bleak, wintery, rural Massachusetts—than for any of her other novels. Still, while *Ethan Frome* is undoubtedly considered a classic American novel, her greatest literary legacy must be her novels of life in late nineteenth-century New York. With an eye at once objective and affectionate, Wharton created a vibrant and compelling fictional world out of a set of life experiences that did nothing to nurture or encourage creativity. Her lasting achievement is that of many great artists—the ability to see something of the universally human in a very specific time and place, to create art out of the commonplace people, places, and things that surrounded her. For this, and for her beautifully written depictions of a unique era in American history, Edith Wharton is counted among America's greatest novelists.

from *The Age of Innocence*

Edith Wharton

She bent over him, laying her hands on his shoulders and looking at him with eyes so deep that he remained motionless under her gaze.

"Ah, don't let us undo what you've done!" she cried. "I can't go back now to that other way of thinking. I can't love you unless I give you up."

His arms were yearning up to her; but she drew away, and they remained facing each other, divided by the distance that her words had created. Then, abruptly, his anger overflowed.

"And Beaufort? Is he to replace me?"

As the words sprang out he was prepared for an answering flare of anger; and he would have welcomed it as fuel for his own. But Madame Olenska only grew a shade paler, and stood with her arms hanging down before her, and her head slightly bent, as her way was when she pondered a question.

"He's waiting for you now at Mrs. Struthers's; why don't you go to him?" Archer sneered.

She turned to ring the bell. "I shall not go out this evening; tell the carriage to go and fetch the Signora Marchesa," she said when the maid came.

After the door had closed again Archer continued to look at her with bitter eyes. "Why this sacrifice? Since you tell me that you're lonely I've no right to keep you from your friends."

She smiled a little under her wet lashes. "I shan't be lonely now. I was lonely; I was afraid. But the emptiness and the darkness are gone; when I turn back into myself now I'm like a child going at night into a room where there's always a light."

A ROMANTIC MEETING
Federigo Andreotti, 1847–?
Fine Art Photographic Library Ltd.

From My Garden Journal

by Deana Deck

HIBISCUS

Unless one lives in a tropical climate, the month of February is difficult to endure. Although spring is just over the horizon, it remains tantalizingly out of sight, and the gray skies and chill winds of winter seem as though they will never depart.

No wonder that Valentine's Day became such a popular event. It's hard to dwell on the weather when you're unwrapping a bouquet of flowers, reading a love note from someone dear, or inhaling the fragrance wafting toward you from a just-opened box of candy. It doesn't matter who the flowers, valentine, or candy are from. In February, it's the thought that counts.

Some thoughts, however, last longer than others. No matter how sweet the sentiment, the valentine will eventually get tossed out, the flowers will wilt, and the candy will dissolve into a memory. No valentine is quite as special or as memory provoking as a blooming plant. Especially one that blooms near-

ly nonstop. The hibiscus (*H. rosasinesis*, which translates to rose of China) is a perfect example.

The hibiscus may be the world's most famous tropical flower. Dorothy Lamour stuck one behind her ear every time she stepped into a sarong. Esther Williams wore them underwater. Fancy hotels from Miami to Maui float them in pools and fountains. In the tropics, you're apt to find one on your pillow at night in place of a foil-wrapped mint.

My first hibiscus was a gift from a friend who had just returned from a trip to Florida. I gave it a place of honor in an east-facing room with sliding glass doors and plenty of light. The plant was covered with glorious red blooms when I received it and seemed content to stay that way. Unbeknownst to me at the time, each blossom on a hibiscus lasts for only a single day but is quickly replaced with another.

When spring came and the days were truly balmy, I moved the plant onto the deck where it got the benefit of a couple of extra hours of sunlight each day. It rejoiced and rewarded me with even more blooms. In the fall, I moved it back indoors, fully expecting it to go dormant, or to at least take a short catnap; but this plant had a one-track mind, and its mind was on blooming.

Now I must admit that I helped it along a little with the proper diet and atmospheric conditions, but I do that with all my plants and none has ever rewarded my efforts so generously. Knowing that blooming plants use up prodigious amounts of energy and stored reserves that need replenishing frequently, I was forced to do some quick research, having never encountered such a prolific bloomer.

HIBISCUS

My task was made easier when I stumbled across a little fact-filled book published by the American Hibiscus Society called *What Every Hibiscus Grower Should Know*. One of the things I learned was that the hibiscus was brought to this country with the first wave of settlers and was greatly prized by George Washington. Another thing is that it comes in a wide array of colors, from brilliant, valentine red to yellow and all shades of pink and white. There are bicolor varieties and single, double, and fringed flower forms.

If you don't live in southern Florida or a similar subtropic climate, the hibiscus must be considered a houseplant. It has a cousin, however, named the Common Rose Mallow (*H. moscheutos*) which is very similar in appearance and does quite well as far north as Boston, Pittsburgh, St. Louis, and on upward along the northwest Pacific coast. It only blooms in summer, but it's quite prolific and beautiful.

In Florida rain falls on the hibiscus plants nearly every day, so it likes moisture. Also, the soil in Florida is very sandy, so the plant drains quickly and doesn't sit around with soggy roots. This is good to remember in the wintertime, because the plant will need frequent watering in a centrally-heated, nontropical home, but it must drain quickly and completely. Just mix a lot of sand in with the plant's soil. Hibiscus also benefits greatly from a daily misting, especially in winter. And, because as you water you are washing nutrients out the drain holes, frequent feeding is highly beneficial.

Frequent feeding leaves the plant vulnerable to salt burn because not all the fertilizer salts dissolve in the soil. Between feedings, be sure you water the plant until the saucer begins to fill. This will help dissolve and leach out harmful salt residue. Empty the saucer immediately.

Like all tropical natives, the hibiscus loves to bask in the sun. Provide it with at least four hours of direct sunlight every day—the more the bet-

I plucked the dead blooms off every day, and my beautiful hibiscus quickly replaced each with a new bloom!

ter. A south window is ideal. And in summer it benefits immensely from a few weeks on the deck or patio.

Now this sounds like you might end up hauling the plant around a lot, but there's good news. The hibiscus does its best blooming when kept slightly pot-bound so you can keep your hibiscus in a manageable container. Don't worry about your potted hibiscus taking after its parents, who were probably fifteen-foot-tall shrubs down in Key West. Being pot-bound is a form of self-bonsai that limits the growth of the plant but doesn't interfere with its ability to bloom.

One word of caution: hibiscus plants are highly susceptible to damage from insecticides. Since they spend the summer outdoors, they're apt to pick up all manner of pesky critters. Keep some insecticidal soap spray handy along with some Bt (Bacillus thuringiensis), a bacterial insecticide that is effective against nearly all chewing caterpillars but not harmful to you, your pets, or the birds and bees.

Even though hibiscus blossoms only last for a day, you can still take advantage of them in arrangements. My favorite way to use them, however, fits right into the whole Valentine's Day scheme of things. Picture, if you will, a quiet dinner at an elegantly set table. Between a set of perfect silver candlesticks is a large crystal bowl and floating on the surface of the water—are those valentines? No, just beautiful hibiscus blossoms in all their tropical glory.

Deana Deck lives in Nashville, Tennessee, where her popular garden column is a regular feature in The Tennessean.

To a Seed Merchant

Edna Jaques

Your catalog arrived today,
Thanks for the cover bright and gay
And all the lovely host it brought—
Delphiniums, forget-me-nots,
Nasturtiums, clustered to one side,
And pale pink roses for a bride.

Although the winter wind is blowing,
Here in my room are flowers growing—
Petunias in their gay attire,
And marigolds like sacred fire,
With Canterbury bells to ring,
Above the tender fields of spring.

Outside my window blizzards rage,
But here upon the glowing page
They smile like lovely guests and oh,
I am so glad that flowers grow
In books. I have them twice you see:
Next summer in the yard
and here tonight
Before the fire with me.

Ideals Anniversary Poem Winner

Ideals would like to extend a heartfelt "Thank You" to all readers who mailed in a poem to be considered in our search for the best anniversary poem. The response was over-whelming—truly a testament to the many talented individuals who read *Ideals* magazine!

ON THE EVE OF THEIR GOLDEN WEDDING DAY

JOHN C. BONSER

"Our Golden Wedding Day draws near,"
   the husband said.
The elderly woman, smiling, raised her head,
"Will you write me a poem as you used to do?
That's the gift I'd like most from you!"

The old man, agreeing, limped from the room,
Went out on the porch in the twilight's gloom,
Leaned on the railing and reminisced:
"Often we sat here, shared hopes, and kissed.

"Dear Lord, how the years have hurried by—
Those memories of youth make an old man sigh!
Now we grow weary and bent and gray,
What clever words can I possibly say

"To show that I love her just as much
As I did when her cheeks were soft to my touch,
When her eyes were bright and her lips were warm,
And we happily walked with her hand on my arm!"

So the husband stood while the evening breeze
Echoed his sigh through the nearby trees
Till the joys they had shared in days long past
Merged into thoughts he could voice at last,

And he went inside and got paper and pen;
Sat down at the kitchen table and then
Carefully wrote what his wife had desired:
A gift as "golden" as a love inspired.

   "Sweetheart, dear wife, my closest friend,
   With you my days begin and end.
   Though time has stolen strength and youth,
   It cannot change this shining truth:
   Our love has lasted all these years
   While hardships came and sorrow's tears.
   We've met each test and gotten by,
   And I will love you till I die!
   We are not rich in worldly wealth
   But we own nothing gained by stealth,
   And you remain my greatest treasure,
   My source of pride and quiet pleasure.
   I wish you all the happiness
   With which two loving hearts are blessed;
   You were, and are, my choice for life,
   My girl, my lady, my sweet wife!"

The poem finished, the husband arose,
Went into the room where his good wife dozed
And tenderly kissing her nodding head,
"Wake up, 'sleeping beauty', and come to bed!"

JOHN C. BONSER, *resident of Florissant, Missouri, has been writing poetry for more than fifty years. He won his first poetry contest while a junior at Beaumont High School in St. Louis, Missouri, and has written off and on ever since. A true romantic, John most often writes poetry for his wife of forty-five years, Betty. John and Betty have four children and six grandchildren.*

Readers' Forum

Meet Our Ideals Readers and Their Families

MARY WIRSING of Lake Clear, New York, snapped this shot of her nephew Jimmy Mertz, here at ten months, as he was helping her unload the clothes basket. Mary and her husband Jack were baby-sitting for the day while Jimmy's parents, Jim and Mariann Mertz, escaped to Lake Placid for a well-deserved day alone together. The Mertzes live in Rensselaer, New York, and welcomed Jimmy's little sister Jamie to the family about one year ago.

Mary enjoyed her mother's subscription so much that she decided to subscribe herself about five years ago. When she's not reading *Ideals*, Mary enjoys gardening, cooking, and crocheting lap robes. The robes are designed specifically for people who use wheelchairs. Mary gives them to area nursing homes to warm the legs and hearts of some of the residents.

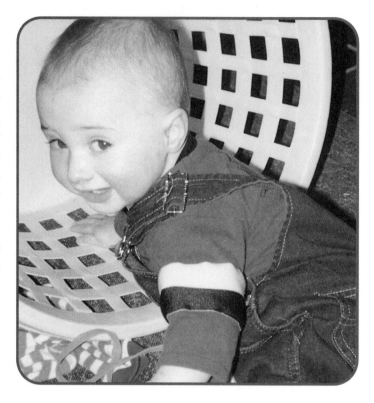

SHIRLEY PFALZGRAF in Lewisville, Ohio, is sure that her grandson, Aaron Lyn Lucas, is saying to himself, "Should I go out and cut more wood or stay in here by the fire?" Quite the little farmer, Aaron, two-and-a-half years old, loves to pull the levers on the automatic log splitter with his Grandpa Jack's help. Aaron also likes to ride with his grandpa on the tractor, the four-wheel drive, or anything else that makes a noise.

Shirley received her first subscription to *Ideals* several years ago as a gift from her daughter (and Aaron's mother), Stacey Lucas. Sometimes she reads them to Aaron as well as her other grandchildren, Robbie, Jennifer, and Jeremy. Not only does Shirley display *Ideals* in her home, but since Stacey has opened a Bed-and-Breakfast inn in Caldwell, Ohio, Shirley even donated some past issues of *Ideals* to display in the rooms.

THANK YOU Mary Wirsing, Shirley Pfalzgraf, and Phyllis Peters for sharing with *Ideals* in this Valentine issue. We hope to hear from other readers who would like to share photos and stories with the *Ideals* family. Please include a self-addressed, stamped envelope if you would like the photos returned. Keep your original photographs for safekeeping and send duplicate photos along with your name, address, and telephone number to:

Readers' Forum
Ideals Publications Inc.
P.O. Box 148000
Nashville, TN 37214-8000

ideals

Publisher, Patricia A. Pingry
Editor, Lisa C. Thompson
Art Director, Patrick McRae
Editorial Assistant, Crystal Edison
Editorial Intern, Heather McArthur
Contributing Editors, Lansing Christman, Deana Deck, Russ Flint, Pamela Kennedy, Mary Skarmeas, Nancy Skarmeas

ACKNOWLEDGMENTS

GIFT BEARING MAN from *LIVING THE YEARS* by Edgar A. Guest, copyright 1949 by The Reilly & Lee Co., used by permission of the author's estate. TO A SEED MERCHANT from *BESIDE STILL WATERS* by Edna Jaques, published in Canada by Thomas Allen & Son Limited. THOU ART LOVELIER THAN LILACS... by Edna St. Vincent Millay, from *COLLECTED POEMS OF EDNA ST. VINCENT MILLAY*, Harper & Row. Copyright 1917, 1945 by Edna St. Vincent Millay. THE LETTER from *LOVE IS A TERRIBLE THING* by Beatrice Murphy, copyright 1949 by Hobson Book Press, used by permission of the author's estate. ONE PERFECT ROSE from *THE PORTABLE DOROTHY PARKER*, copyright 1926, renewed 1954 by Dorothy Parker. Reprinted by permission of Viking Penguin, an imprint of Penguin USA. Our sincere thanks to the following authors whom we were unable to contact: E.O. Boyle for STRANGE THAT SUCH A LITTLE ROSE; Charles Divine for WE MET ON ROADS OF LAUGHTER; Reginald Holmes for MY VALENTINE; Alice Johnson for BEST VALENTINE; and Florence S. Reed for SKATING PARTY.

PHYLLIS PETERS of Three Rivers, Michigan, sent us this photograph of her great-grandson Blaine Ayotte. Phyllis wrote to us: "I find your publications eliminate any generation gap. Blaine and I sit together and leaf through the pages, enjoying the beauitiful pictures as I read to him." Blaine's mother, Tamara Ayotte, lives in Three Rivers as well, so visits between grandmother, granddaughter, and great-grandson can be often.

Forty years ago, Phyllis's neighbor, a retired schoolteacher, introduced her to *Ideals* when Phyllis was a young mother. She says she has missed very few issues in the meantime, during which she became the mother of two, grandmother of five, and now great-grandmother of three. Phyllis is a senior citizen who likes to stitch log cabin quilt designs, crochet, and write on a freelance basis for magazines and newspapers. What she enjoys most of all, however, is probably baby-sitting!

Gold Flowers in the Snow

Beverly J. Anderson

CROCUSES OF GOLD.
Superstock, Inc.

Yesterday it was wintertime;
Snow covered all the ground.
The wind blew cold, and springtime was
Just nowhere to be found.

My soul felt winter-weary, and
The spring seemed far away.
Then suddenly, a miracle
Before my eyes—today!

I saw some brave young crocuses
Had pushed through icy snow,
And cheery sunbeams greeted them
And set them all aglow.

A sight so beautiful to see,
A joy my heart to know;
When spring and winter mingled
brought
Gold flowers in the snow.

Oh, tiny precious crocuses,
Emerged from winter's sod,
I think that surely you must be
A special gift from God!

Statement of ownership, management, and circulation (Required by 39 U.S.C. 3685), of Ideals, published eight times a year in February, March, May, June, August, September, November, and December at Nashville, Tennessee, for September 1994. Publisher, Patricia A. Pingry; Editor, Lisa C. Thompson; Managing Editor, as above; Owner, Ideals Publications Incorporated, 565 Marriott Drive #800, Nashville, TN 37214. Stockholders: Simon Waterlow, President, Martin Flanagan, Vice President, and Patricia A. Pingry, Vice President, 565 Marriott Drive #800, Nashville, TN 37214. Known bondholders, mortgages, and other security holders: Egmont Foundation, VOGNMAGERGADE II, 1148 Copenhagen, K. Denmark and Trans Financial Bank, P.O. Box 3490, 1816 Madison Street, Clarksville, TN 37043. Average no. copies each issue during preceding 12 months: Total no. copies printed (Net Press Run) 179,649. Paid circulation 31,582. Mail subscription 137,647. Total paid circulation 169,229. Free distribution 355. Total distribution 169,584. Actual no. copies of single issue published nearest to filing date: Total no. copies printed (Net Press Run) 143,881. Paid circulation 10,779. Mail subscription 125,955. Total paid circulation 136,734. Free distribution 192. Total distribution 136,926. I certify that the statements made by me above are correct and complete. Rose A. Yates, Vice President, Direct Marketing Systems and Operations.